Claws

Jan Burchett and Sara Vogler ● Jonatronix

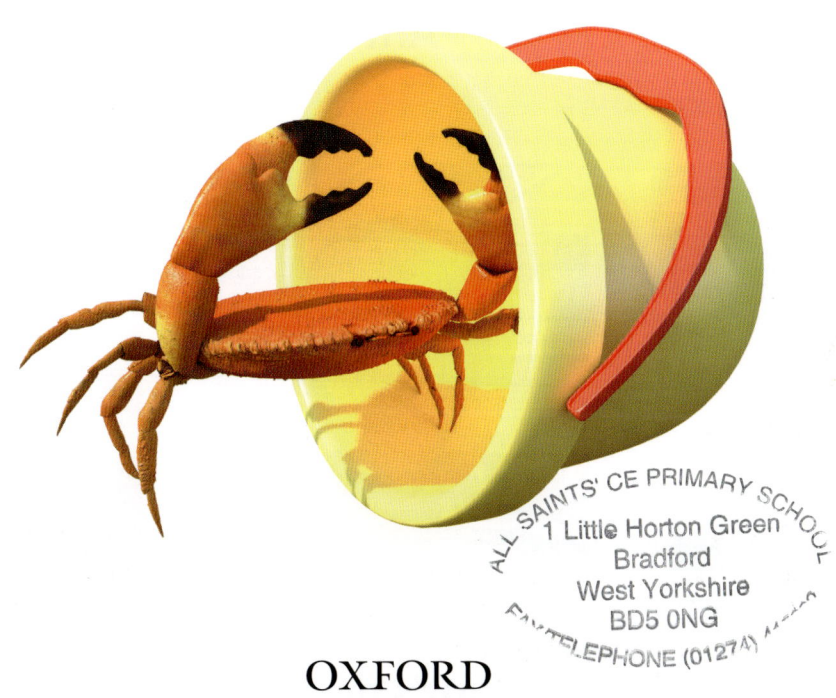

OXFORD
UNIVERSITY PRESS

In this story ...

Cat

Ant

Nok

Ant's mum

Ant's dad

crab

Cat and Ant were enjoying a day at the beach with Nok. Ant's mum and dad were having a nap.

Cat and Ant went to play near the
rock pools.
"I have found a big crab!" cried Ant.
"Let's put it in the bucket," said Cat.

As Cat bent down, their bucket fell on to the rocks. The splash from the bucket hit Ant's arm.

A beam shot out and hit the crab.
The crab got bigger and bigger.

The crab's sharp claws were snapping.
Nok ran and hid underneath a big
blue seashell.

Cat had to clamber across the rocks
to get away.
Ant tried to get away too but he slid
on some seaweed.

The crab lifted Ant up in its claw. It went scuttling off.

The crab darted across the rocks.
It held on tight to Ant.
"Help!" he cried.

"People will see the crab!" Cat cried.
"You need to shrink."
Ant tried, but the crab kept scuttling about.

In the end, Ant hit the button. He shrank ... and the crab shrank too.

Cat put the crab in the bucket. Then she found Nok under the blue seashell.

Ant went back to normal. Then he saw his mum and dad.

"Oh, that's a big crab!" cried Mum, looking into their bucket.
"We have seen a much bigger crab than this today," replied Cat, grinning.

Retell the story